D1420862

X-TREME LATIN

X-TREME LATIN

LINGUA LATINA EXTREMA

All the Latin you need to know for surviving the 21st century

HENRY BEARD
HENRICUS BARBATUS

headline

Copyright © 2004 Henry Beard

The right of Henry Beard to be identified as the Author of the Work has been asserted by him in accordance with the Copyright, Designs and Patents Act 1988.

First published in 2004 by
Gotham Books, a division of Penguin Group (USA) Inc.

First published in Great Britain in 2004 by
HEADLINE BOOK PUBLISHING

10 9 8 7 6 5 4 3 2 1

All rights reserved. Apart from any use permitted under UK copyright law, this publication may only be reproduced, stored, or transmitted, in any form, or by any means, with prior permission in writing of the publishers or, in the case of reprographic production, in accordance with the terms of licences issued by the Copyright Licensing Agency.

Every effort has been made to fulfil requirements with regard to reproducing copyright material. The author and publisher will be glad to rectify any omissions at the earliest opportunity.

Cataloguing in Publication Data is available from the British Library

ISBN 0 7553 1295 3

Illustrations by Valerie Baker

Designed by Viv Mullett

Typeset in Dante MT by Avon DataSet Ltd, Bidford-on-Avon, Warks
Printed and bound in Great Britain by
Clays Ltd St Ives plc

Headline's policy is to use papers that are natural, renewable and recyclable products and made from wood grown in sustainable forests. The logging and manufacturing processes are expected to conform to the environmental regulations of the country of origin.

HEADLINE BOOK PUBLISHING
A division of Hodder Headline
338 Euston Road
London NW1 3BH

www.headline.co.uk
www.hodderheadline.com

Contents
INDEX CAPITUM

Author's Note ix
Preface xi

I. BEGINNING LATIN

A Little Story 3
Latin Aptitude Test 5
Romulus and Remus Jokes 7
The Legion of Superheroes 10
T-shirt Slogans 11
Bumper Stickers 13
Reality TV 15
Hardball Talk Shows 17
Ultimate Sports 18
Trash Talk in the Colosseum 21
Spring Break 24
Country Music Favorites 25
Chilling Out 27
Graffiti 28
Road Rage 31
Air Rage 34
Warning Labels 35

II. INTERMEDIATE LATIN

Caesar's PowerPoint Presentation 39
Top 10 Reasons to Live in the Time of the Caesars 42
That Old-Time Religion 44
Mob Banter 47
New Age Discourse 49
Hollywood Latin 50
Sushi Bar Chitchat 52
Computer Language 54
Car Talk 55
B.S. 57
Small Talk During a Colonoscopy 60
Medical Confab 61
Homeland Security 63
Useful Phrases for Barbarian Evildoers 64
Game Boy Chatter 66
Modern Vatican Latin 68
Learned Latin for Lovers 70
Classical Kiss-offs 73

III. ADVANCED LATIN

Useful Syntax 77
You Know You May Be a Roman If . . . 82
Restaurant 'Tude 85
Winespeak 87
The Bestseller List 89
Latin for Trekkies 91
Attack Ads 93
Business Latin 94

Let the Buyer Go Mad 96
Jury Duty 98
Stealth Latin 101
Stealth Latin for Golfers 104
Bad Latin, the Dirty Dozen 106

Author's Note

Although I did the original Latin composition for the first draft of this book, my translations have been extensively corrected, meticulously polished, and felicitously rephrased by J. Mark Sugars, Ph.D., without whose assistance I would have been in *merda profundissima* (very deep doo-doo). Thus, to the extent that the classical constructions herein are historically appropriate, grammatically accurate, and culturally apt, it is he who deserves the imposing, but tasteful, triumphal arch on the sunny side of the Forum, just below the Palatine Hill. If, however, there are any *errata ignominiosa* (cock ups), it is I and I alone who should be exiled to the remote, windswept tip of some godforsaken island inhabited by rude barbarians. (The Hamptons will do nicely.)

That said, I have to confess that even the most dedicated Latin purist inevitably succumbs to the temptation to make a cheap joke at the expense of the noble tongue of Rome's golden age, and I am no exception. Therefore, in the interests of scholarly integrity, I am compelled to concede that there is no Latin verb *'geronimo, geronimare'* meaning 'to express an intention to act boldly or rashly,' say, just prior to jumping off a bridge, and if a Roman diner wished to remark, 'I will recommend this restaurant,' *'zago, zagas, zagat'* is not the way he would have phrased it. The rest of the Augustan yadda-yadda (*'iaddo, iaddere, iaddedi, iadditum'*) is as kosher as we could make it.

Oh, all right. Yadda-yadda is actually *blatero, blaterare.* Sheesh.

Preface
PRAEFATIO
PRY-FAH-TIH-OH

It's often said that Latin is a dead language
Lingua Latina saepe dicitur mortua esse
LEEN-gwah lah-TEE-nah SIGH-pay DEE-kih-tuhr MOHR-too-ah EHS-seh

Bollocks!
Coleus!
Koh-LEE-uhs!

It's just been taking a long nap
Modum iam pridem meridiatur
MOH-duhm yahm PREE-dehm meh-ree-dih-AH-tuhr

And it's been talking a lot in its sleep
Iam diu autem multa verba facit dormiens
Yahm DIH-ooh OW-tehm MOOL-tah WEHR-bah FAH-kiht DOHR-mih-ehns

In fact, you can't get it to shut up
Re vera, non potes eam in silentium redigere
Ray WAY-rah nohn POH-tess EH-ahm ihn sih-LAYN-tih-uhm reh-DIHG-eh-reh

Look around – Latin is all over the place, like a cheap toga

Circumspice – Lingua Latina se pandit ubique tanquam toga vilis

KEER-kuhm-spih-keh – LEEN-gwah lah-TEE-nah say PAHN-diht ooh-BEE-kweh TAHN-kwaum TOH-gah WIH-liss

Lawyers use it to screw you

Iurisperiti ea utuntur ut te defraudent

Yoo-riss-peh-REE-tee EH-ah uh-TOON-tuhr uht tay deh-FROW-dehnt

Doctors use it to scare you shitless

Medici hac lingua utuntur ut alvum evacues ex metu

MEH-dih-kee hock LEEN-gwah uh-TOON-tuhr uht AHL-wuhm ay-WAH-koo-ays eks MEH-tooh

Politicians use it to hide their tracks while they rob you blind

Magistratus ea utuntur ad operienda vestigia cum te despoliant

Mah-gihs-TRAH-toohs EH-ah uh-TOON-tuhr ahd oh-pehr-ih-AYN-dah wehs-TEE-gih-ah kuhm tay deh-SPOH-lih-ahnt

Priests use it to weasel their way out when they get caught playing hide-the-sausage with the altar boys

Sacerdotes in stupro cum acolytis deprehensi ea utuntur ut se criminibus absolvant

Sah-kehr-DOH-tays ihn STOOP-roh kuhm ah-koh-LEE-teese day-preh-HAYN-see EH-ah uh-TOON-tuhr uht say krih-MIHN-ih-buhss ahb-SOHL-wahnt

Even garden supply stores use it to get you to buy overpriced, short-lived houseplants

Etiam venditores rerum hortensium ea utuntur ad persuadendum tibi ut emas maximo pretio plantas vitae brevis

EH-tih-ahm wehn-dih-TOHR-ace RAY-ruhm hohr-TAYN-sih-uhm EH-ah uh-TOON-tuhr ahd pehr-swah-DAYN-duhm TIH-bee uht EH-mahs MAHK-sih-moh PREH-tih-oh PLAHN-tahs WEE-tye BREH-wihss

The fact is, for too long these dirtbags have had a monopoly on this mighty tongue

Diutius quidem haec propudia monopolio huius magnifici sermonis fruuntur

Dih-OO-tih-uhs KWIH-dehm hike proh-POOH-dih-ah moh-noh-POH-lih-oh HOO-eeh-uhss mahg-NIH-fih-kee sehr-MOH-nihss frooh-OON-tuhr

But now, thanks to this little book, you too can tap the awesome power of Latin to dismay the ignorant multitudes

Nunc vero, huius libelli gratia, tu quoque potentia reverenda linguae Latinae uti potes ad indoctum vulgus consternandum

Nuhnk WAY-roh, HOO-eeh-uhss lih-BEHL-lee GRAH-tih-ah, too KWOH-kweh poh-TAYN-tih-ah reh-weh-RAYN-dah LEEN-gwigh LAH-tih-nigh OO-tee POH-tehss ahd ihn-DOHK-tuhm WUHL-guhs kohn-stehr-NAHN-duhm

And best of all, you'll be able to insult and abuse one and all in perfect safety, using a language that everyone respects but practically no one understands

Atque haec est optima ratio omnium: maledicere cunctis hominibus et contumeliam imponere satis impune poteris verbis augustis quae cum omnes magno aestimant, tum nemo ferme intellegit

AHT-kweh hike ehst OHP-tih-mah RAH-tih-oh OHM-nih-uhm: mah-leh-DEEK-eh-reh KOONK-tees hoh-MIHN-ih-buhss eht kohn-tuh-MAY-lih-ahm ihm-POH-neh-reh SAH-tihss ihm-POO-neh poh-TEH-rihss WAYR-beese ow-GOOS-teese kwy kuhm OHM-nays MAHG-noh EYE-stih-mahnt tuhm NEH-mo FAYR-meh ihn-TEHL-leh-giht

And as you pepper your speech with catapult-powered put-downs, remember the immortal words of Maximus as he signaled the attack in Pannonia:

Itaque cum spargis orationem tuam praepotentibus opprobriis, memento verborum immortalium quae Maximus fecit signum dans in Pannonia:

Ih-TAH-kweh kuhm SPAHR-ghiss oh-rah-tih-OH-nehm TOO-ahm prigh-poh-TAYN-tih-buhss ohp-PROH-brih eehs, meh-MEHN-toh wayr-BOH-ruhm ihm-mohr-TAH-lih-uhm kwigh MAHK-sih-muhss FAY-kiht SIHG-nuhm dahns ihn Pahn-NOH-nih-ah:

Unleash hell!

Solve lora infernis!

SOHL-weh LOH-rah ihn-FEHR-nihss!

And have a nice day!

Et futue te ipsum!

Eht FUH-too-eh tay IHP-suhm

Latin Terms in Modern English

LEGAL LATIN

Latin word or phrase	*English meaning*
in flagrante delicto habeas corpus prima facie nolo contendere res ipsa loquitur	you're in big trouble

MEDICAL LATIN

Latin word or phrase	*English meaning*
macula fistula carcinoma angina medulla oblongata	you're dead

POLITICAL LATIN

Latin word or phrase	*English meaning*
pro forma ex officio per diem sine qua non quid pro quo	the fix is in

ECCLESIASTICAL LATIN

Latin word or phrase	*English meaning*
ex cathedra in pectore urbi et orbi in hoc signo vinces sic transit gloria mundi	the bishop is not available

BOTANICAL LATIN

Latin word or phrase	*English meaning*
grandiflora tomentosa pendula rugosa sempervirens	leafless clump of dry brown twigs in one week flat

Basic Latin Pronunciation Guide

VOWELS

a	if long, as in 'bl*ah*'; if short, as in 'rub-*a*-dub'
e	if long, as in 'ol*é*'; if short as in '*feh*'
i	if long, as in ''z*i*ne'; if short as in 'z*i*t'
o	if long, as in 'd'*oh*'; if short as in 'n*o*t'
u	if long, as in 'd*u*de'; if short as in 'wass*u*p'

There is really no simple way to tell if a vowel is long or short, but if the word is short – one syllable – treat the vowel as short. The last syllable of verb endings are almost always short. If *a, i, o,* or *u,* come at the end of a word, they're long; if *e* comes at the end of a word, it's short. If a vowel is followed by two consonants, it's long. For other situations, pronuntia utrolibet modo! (wing it!)

DIPTHONGS

ae	as in 'Th*ai*'
au	as in '*ou*ch'
ei	as in 'h*ey*'
eu	as in 'h*ey*, y*ou*'
oe	as in 'g*oy*'
ui	as in 'pt*ui*'

CONSONANTS

b, d, f, h, l, m, n, and *p* are the same as in English. So are *k* and *z,* which are rare in Latin anyway. *j, w,* and the consonant *y* don't exist in Latin.

c, ch always 'k.' That's a KIGH-sahr salad you ordered. You want ANN-koh-veese with that?

g, gn always 'guh.' The Romans were fighting the GUHR-mahns, not the JUR-mahns, and when they gave the signal to attack, it was a SIHG-nuhm (trumpet blast) not a SEE-nuhm (large bowl).

i always 'yuh.' It's thanks to YOO-lih-uhss (not JOO-lee-yuss) that we celebrate the fourth of July instead of the fourth of Quinctil.

r you can rrroll your r's even if they'rrre the last letterrr of a worrrrd.

s always 'sss.' The Roman fanss (not fanz) were animalss (not animalz).

t, th always 'teh.' Teh-hey teh-rew teh-hings at eak otteh-her during teh-he nah-tih-oh-nahl (not nashunal) ant-hem (not anthum).

v always 'w.' The wolcano that waporized Pompeii was Weh-SOO-wee-uhss.

There are no silent letters in Latin – every vowel (unless it's part of a two-syllable dipthong) and every consonant is always pronounced fully, and often separately. Of course, there are also no actual Romans around to sneer when you mess up.

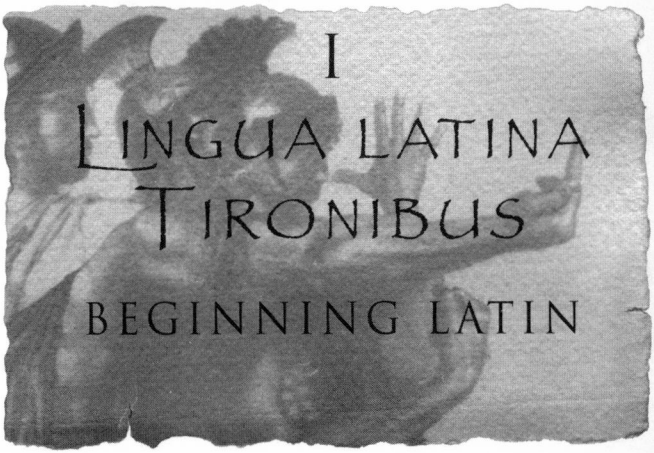

I

Lingua Latina Tironibus

BEGINNING LATIN

A Little Story
NARRATIUNCULA

Puellae filiae agricolarum sunt
The girls are the daughters of the farmers

Puellae pulchrae sunt
The girls are pretty

Puellae nautas in via spectant
The girls see the sailors in the street

Nautae pulchri sunt
The sailors are hunks

Puellae nautas salutant
The girls say hello to the sailors

O malam fortunam! Nautae male mares sunt
Too bad! The sailors are homos

Nautae ad puellas digitos impudicos porrigunt
The sailors give the girls the finger

Puellae nautas appellant
The girls call out to the sailors

'Speramus naviculam misellam vestram ad scopulum adlisam iri summersum'
'We hope your stupid boat hits a rock and sinks'

Puellae in forum descendere destinant et ibi mercimonium furari
The girls decide to go down to the mall and shoplift some stuff

Omnes paucis annis prosedae erunt
In a few years they will all be hookers

Latin Aptitude Test
PROBATIO LATINITATIS

(answers below – *responsa recta in ima pagina*)

I. MATH – SCIENTIA MATHEMATICA

All Gaul is divided into ___ parts
Gallia est omnis divisa in partes ___

A. many
multas

B. good
bonas

C. small
parvas

D. warlike
bellicosas

E. Capture a Gaul and torture him until he tells you
Torque Gallum captum donec tibi respondeat

II. VERBAL – SCIENTIA VERBORUM

Arms and the man I sing, who first from the shores of ___ . . .
Arma virumque cano ___ qui primus ab oris . . .

A. Syracuse
Syracusarum
B. Ithaca
Ithacae
C. Albany
Albani
D. Buffalo
Bufali
E. Sacrifice a bullock to Jupiter so the test gets canceled because the teacher was struck by lightning
Immola Iovi iuvencum ut magistro tacto de caelo probatio relinquatur

III. EXTRA CREDIT – QUAESTIO ADDITA PRAEMII GRATIA

Whatever it is, I fear the Greeks even when bearing _____

Quidquid id est, timeo Danaos et _____ ferentes

A. shish kebabs
carunculas veribus fixas
B. stuffed grape leaves
folia vitis oryza farta
C. baklava
crustula laminosa
D. the check
syngrapham
E. Send a slave over later with the answer, and if he gets it wrong, lop off his ears
Mitte brevi postea servum qui responsum referat atque si erret praecide aures ei

I., E; II, E; III, E.

Romulus and Remus Jokes

ROMULI REMIQUE IOCULARIA

ROMULUS: Why did the sacred chicken cross the Appian Way?

ROMULUS: Quem ob rem pullus sacer viam Appiam transivit?

REMUS: I do not know. Let us cut it open and see if the entrails provide an explanation for this inauspicious behaviour!

REMUS: Nescio. Eum evisceremus ut, extane ostensura sint illius infausti facti causam, comperiamus!

ROMULUS: Why do Roman firemen wear red braces?

ROMULUS: Cur gerunt siphonarii Romani retinacula rubra?

REMUS: I do not know – let us set the city ablaze and see if their trousers fall down!

REMUS: Nescio. Urbem incendamus ut, sintne delapsurae bracae eorum, comperiamus!

ROMULUS: Why did the Helvetian moron throw the water clock out the window?

ROMULUS: Quare iecit caudex Helvetius clepsydram de fenestra?

REMUS: I do not know, but I feel certain that after ten years chained to an oar as a galley slave he will be eager to reveal the reason for his rash act!

REMUS: Nescio; pro certo tamen habeo istum, decem annos vinctum in servitio ad remum intra navem longam, cupidum futurum revelare rationem sui temerarii facti!

Why do Roman firemen wear red braces?
Cur gerunt siphonarii Romani retinacula rubra?
I do not know – let us set the city ablaze and see if their trousers fall down!
Nescio. Urbem incendamus ut, sintne delapsurae bracae eorum, comperiamus!

The Legion of Superheroes
LEGIO HEROUM MAXIMORUM

Faster than a speeding chariot . . .
Celerior quam currus festinans . . .

More powerful than a Carthaginian war-elephant . . .
Valentior quam elephas bellicus Punicus . . .

Able to conjugate irregular verbs without making a single mistake . . .
Potis anomala verba sine lapsu declinare . . .

It's Ro-Man!
Romanus est!

T-shirt Slogans
TITULI TUNICALES

CARPE NAREM
Pick your nose

CAPE SOMNUM
Catch some 'z's'

CAPIAMUS CEREVISIAM
Let's grab a beer

CAVE LABOREM
Beware of work

MORANS FAC PAUSAM UT SEDES BIROTARUM OLFACIAS
Take time to stop and smell the bicycle seats

PUTEO ERGO SUM
I stink, therefore I am

VENI, VIDI, VOMUI
I came, I saw, I blew lunch

SOLVE LORA INFERNIS
Unleash hell

OSTENDE MIHI PECUNIAM
Show me the money

PARENTES MEI DIMIDIUM EUROPAE DESPOLIA VERUNT. EGO TAMEN NIL ACCEPI PRAETER HANC TUNICULAM MISELLAM
My parents plundered half of Europe and all I got was this stupid T-shirt

ABES ETIAM A CONSILIO INSULTANDI MIHI NISI LATINE LOQUI SCIAS
Don't even think of dissing me unless you speak Latin

ILLUC IVI, ILLUD FECI
Been there, done that

Bumper Stickers
TITULI CURRULES

I'd rather be pillaging
Malim praedari

I'm dumb and I vote
Hebes sum et suffragia fero

My child can beat the crap out of your wimpy honor student
Filius meus puerum tuum studiosum laureatum mollem deverberare potest

Thank you for not thanking me for not smoking
Tibi gratias ago quod mihi gratias non agis quod fumum non comedo

Visualize world conquest
Habe ante oculos devictionem mundi

Keep honking – I'm reloading
Perge cornu canere – sclopetum repleo

Horn broken – watch for finger
Buccina fracta – exspecta signum digiti impudici

Barbarian on board
Barbarus in curru

Proud of our brutal police
Vigilitus nostris crudelibus gloriantes

Stop the aqueduct, save the unicorns
Sistite constructionem aquaeductus ut conservetis unicornes

I brake for lunch
Frenos inhibere soleo pransurus

Don't blame me – I voted for Miss Piggy
Nolite me culpare – Suffragatus sum Erae Porcellae

Jesus loves you – everyone else thinks you're an asshole
Te amat Iesus – ceteri te putant irrumatorem

If you can read this, I lost my trailer
Si hoc potes legere, traheam meam amisi

Reality TV
SPECTACULA TELEVISORIA VERI SIMILIA

Celebrity Shark Attack
Impetus Pistricum in Insignes

Supermodel Food Fight
Pulcherrimae Inter Se Luctantes Edulibus

Beach Babe Lapdance Showdown
Certamen Ultimum Saltandi Nympharum Litoralium in Genibus Virorum

Blow Job Island
Insula Fellatoria

Nationwide Red Alert Hot Bod Strip Search
Inquisitio Summa Cum Vigilantia Per Omnes Nationis Partes Diffusa Corporum Formosiorum Nudatorum

Meet the Organ Donors
Salvete, O Daturi Membra Post Mortem

Baby-sitters from Hell Bring Home Animals that Kill for Fun
Nutriculae Infernales in Domos Adducunt Feras Quae ad Delicias Interficiunt

Big Fat Slobs Eat Shit for Cash
Helluones Squalidi Merdam Pro Nummis Comedunt

Who Wants to Marry a Rich Old Fart with a Terminal Disease?
Quis Vult Nubere Peditori Capulari Diviti?

Hardball Talk Shows
DISCEPTATIONES TUMULTUOSAE

That's a load of bull, and you know it!
Merae fabulae sunt, et eas esse tales scis!

You wouldn't know a fact if one hit you on the head!
Rem veram non cognoscas etiamsi frontem tibi feriat!

You're a liberal stooge!
Pedisequus parasiticus es popularium!

You're a right-wing moron!
Stipator stultus es optimatum!

See you next week!
Vos revisemus post septimanam!

Ultimate Sports
LUDI EXTRAORDINARII

Bass-fishing – Piscatus Percarum

Let me guess – you have to drink the beer to make room in the ice chest for all the fish you catch

Ut coniecturam faciam – necesse est tibi bibere cerevisiam ut locum in cista glaciei des piscibus captis

It's a keeper!

Licet mihi hunc retinere!

Stock car racing – Certamen Curruum Generalium

When are they going to start running into each other and blowing up?

Quando inter se collidentes incipient in flammas dirumpi?

Pit stop!

Statio restaurativa!

Wrestling – Luctatus

Something tells me that the mean-looking bearded guy dressed up like the Ayatollah is no match for the wily Captain America

Suspicor illum truculentum barbatum ritu archierei Persici vestitum non esse comparem Centurioni Americano vafro

Smashmouth! Smackdown!

Ictus in os! Prostratio!

Bungee jumping – Saltus de Ponte

How dumb would you have to be to jump off a bridge with a rope tied to your foot?

Quam vecors sit is qui de ponte saliat pedibus funiculo ligatis?

Geronimo!

Geronimo, geronimare!

Snowboarding – Super Nivem Labi

Hey dude, let's head to the halfpipe, catch some major air, and stick some tricks!

Heus, laute, contendamus ad canalem nivalem ut aerem oppido capientes nonnullas technas exsequamur!

Super rad! I'm stoked!

Maxime radicitus! Flagro!

The Olympics – Olympia

I'll vote for the Greek in the wrestling if you vote for the Roman in the chariot race

Graeco palmam dabo in certamine luctandi si Romano palmam dabis in certamine quadrigarum

Deal!

Fiat haec pactio!

Trash Talk in the Colosseum

CONTUMELIA IN AMPHITHEATRO FLAVIO

You want a part of me? Bring it on!
Visne partem mei capere? Comminus agamus!

Are you dissing me?
Insultasne tu miki?

You're yesterday's news
In actis diurnis iamdudum es celebratus

You're toast
Mox corvos pasces

You don't know your ass from a catacomb
Non possis distinguere tuum podicem a Puticulis

Your mother is so fat, when she's in town, Rome has eight hills
Mater tua tam obesa est ut cum Romae est, urbs habet octo colles

Your mother is so ugly, when the gods turned her into a pig, she thought her prayers had been answered
Mater tua tam turpis est ut cum di eam mutaverint in porcam, suas preces putaverit eos audivisse

Your mother is so stupid, when she found a coin with Caesar's name on it, she tried to return it to him

Mater tua tam stulta est ut cum invenerit nummum ferentem nomen Caesaris, huic eum restituere conata sit

Go ahead, punk – make my day

Age, catamite – fac mihi hunc diem felicissimum

Your mother is so fat, when she's in town, Rome has eight hills
Mater tua tam obesa est ut cum Romae est, urbs habet octo colles
Kiss my basilisk
Basia basiliscum meum

Spring Break
FERIAE VERNALES

Road trip!
Iter faciamus!

Let's party hearty!
Pergraecemur!

Wet T-shirt contest!
Certamen inter mammosas tunicis madefactis vestitas!

Go ahead, ask for proof of age. See, I've got a Latin ID. I'm 2,000 years old.
Age, scrutare chartam identitatis meam. Ecce, est mihi syngraphus Latinus. Duo milia annorum sum natus.

I'm wasted!
Crapulentus sum!

I'm going to throw up!
Vomiturus sum!

Country Music Favourites
MUSICA RUSTICA FAVORABILISSIMA

Si Telephonium Non Tintinnat, Ego Voco
If Your Phone Doesn't Ring, It's Me

Causam Tibi Dabo Bibendi
I'll Give You Something to Drink About

Quomodo Una Nocte Facta Tam Turpis Es?
How Did You Get So Ugly Overnight?

Si Dies Hodiernus Esset Piscis, Reicerem
If Today Was a Fish I'd Throw it Back

Mater Cape Malleum, Musca Sedet in Capite Patris
Mother Get the Hammer, There's a Fly on Papa's Head

Si Me Deseras, Liceatne Mihi Te Comitari?
If You Leave Me, Can I Come Too?

Quomodo Te Desiderare Potero Si Non Discesseris?
How Can I Miss You If You Won't Go Away?

Per Anulum Illa Trusit Digitum Medicinalem, Ac Ostendit Mihi Digitum Medium
She Got the Ring, and I Got the Finger

Tu Causa Es Cur Liberi Nostri Tam Turpiculi Sint
You're the Reason Our Kids Are So Ugly

Sine Te Tam Miser Sum Ut Videaris Etiamnunc Adesse
I'm So Miserable Without You It's Like Having You Here

Caput Dolet, Pedes Fetent, Iesum Non Amo
My Head Hurts, My Feet Stink, and I Don't Love Jesus

Chilling Out
SERMO OTIOSORUM

Wassup?
Quagis?

Nothin', watching the game
Nihil ago, ludos specto

True, true
Vero, vero

It's off the hook
Ab unco remotumst

Talk to the hand, the face don't understand
Adloquere manum, facies nescit quid velis

Black togas are cool
Togae atrae lepidae sunt

Want to see my sword collection?
Vin' aspicere collectum gladiorum meum?

I'm thinking of taking a catapult into the school cafeteria . . .
Cogito ferre catapultam in cenationem scholae . . .

Graffiti
INSCRIPTIONES LATRINALES

Make love, not war – hell, get married, do both
Suscipite amorem, non bellum – eheu, iuncti matrimonio, suscipite utrumque

Procrastinate now
Procrastina rem nunc

Flush twice, it's a long way to Texas
Evacua cratera latrinalem bis, Texas procul est

If it has tits, tyres, or testicles, it's nothing but trouble
Mammeatae, rotalia, testiculati, omni modo molesta sunt

Gods are dead
Di mortui sunt

Beauty is in the eye of the beer-holder
Cervesia pota, pulchritudo cernitur

Yankee, go home – and take me with you
Americani, redite domum – ducentes me vobiscum

If we aren't supposed to eat animals, why are they made of meat?
Si quidem animalia nobis edenda non sunt, quare constant ex carne?

There are three kinds of people: those who can count, and those who can't
Sunt genera tria hominum: illi qui numerare possunt, et illi qui non possunt

It *is* as bad as you think, and they *are* out to get you
Res tam malae sunt quam putas, et inimici re vera te persequuntur

Why don't psychics ever win the lottery?
In sortitionibus donativis, cur numquam praemia consequuntur sortilegi?

Aunt Em: Hate you, Hate Kansas, Taking the dog – Dorothy
Amita Aemilia: Te Kansiamque odi, Canem mecum abduco – Dorothea

If walking is so good for you, why does my mailman look like Jabba the Hut?
Si quidem pedibus ire tam salubre corpori est, cur similis est noster tabellarius forma illi Iabbae Hutico?

Kill Barney
Interfice Arcturulum, istum mimum personatum portentosum purpureum palaeozoicum

That's it, numbnuts. Pull out in front of me, then slow down when you get to the light
Euge, enervate eunuche! Ingredere in orbitam meam prae me, tum reprime cursum cum biviali lucernae approprinquas
Where did you learn to drive – fleeing from the Huns?
Ubi didicisti gubernare currum? In fuga ab Hunnis?

Road Rage
IRA IN VIA

Where did you learn to drive – fleeing from Huns?
Ubi didicisti gubernare currum? In fuga ab Hunnis?

That's it, numbnuts. Pull out in front of me, then slow down when you get to the light.
Euge, enervate eunuche! Ingredere in orbitam meam prae me, tum reprime cursum cum biviali lucernae approprinquas.
Now speed up when I try to pass you, and as I go by, give me the finger
Nunc, accelera cum conor te praeterire, mihique praetereunti ostende digitum impudicum

Okay, tailgater – time for a brake check
Em, ichneumon – tempus est sufflamina temptare

Big car, little dick
Currus magnus, mentula minuscula

You know what S.U.V.s and hemorrhoids have in common? Every asshole has one.
Scisne quid commune superlativa urbana vehicula cum haemorrhoidis habeant? Est unum ex his utrisque malis cuique pathico.

Lady, if you're going to sit there all day yakking on your mobile, why don't you stick a steering wheel on your living room wall and just stay home?

Muliercula, si vis ibi sedens garrire totum diem in Nokiam tuam, quidni rotam adfigens gubernalem ad murum conclavis domi maneas?

What are you saving those pretty little turn signals for – Christmas?

Quod ad tempus reservas ista lumina pulchella praemonitoria – ad Saturnalia?

No, Mr Busybody, I am not handicapped, but you will be if you don't move your nosy butt out of that parking place, pronto

Minime, ardelio, nullo modo debilis sum, sed fies tu quidem, si clunes tuas curiosas non removeris protinam ab illa statione

Don't clamp my car!

Noli caligam in rotam currus mei adfigere!

I am too allowed in the car pool lane! See, I'm not alone. I suffer from multiple personality disorder.

Certe mihi licet vehi in orbita seposita curribus repletis. Ecce, non solus sum. Legio mihi nomen est, quia multi sumus.

There are three of us here. I want to drive! No, it's my turn! Not fair, what about me? Me me me!

Adsunt tres. Volo gubernare! Immo, ordo memet vocat! Iniquum est! Quid de me? Me me me!

Does that Breathalyzer have a Latin setting?

Potestne illa machina pneumatodocimastica ad linguam Latinam accommodari?

I have Vatican diplomatic immunity. If you give me a ticket, you're going to end up cooling your heels in The Hague in a jail cell full of Yugoslavian war criminals.

Sedes Romana Sacra mihi diplomaticam immunitatem tribuit. Si me vocaveris in ius, aetatem tuam deges Hagae Comitis, conditus in carcerem refertum Iugoslavorum condemnatorum de bellum contra ius gentium gerendo.

Air Rage
IRA IN AËRE

Do you have nail-clipper-sniffing dogs?
Habetisne canes quae forficulas unguales olfacere possunt?

I think that guy with a napkin on his noggin has a catapult in his shoe
Credo illum mantelium in capite gerentem occultavisse catapultam in caliga

Hey, pal, is that carry-on luggage or did you just sack Carthage?
Heia, amice, utrum illae sunt sarcinae tuae, an modo Carthaginem despoliasti?

Say, miss, didn't you used to work for Con Air?
Dic mihi, domnicella, nonne te conducebat aëria classis quae condemnatos transportabat?

You know, even galley slaves were served meals
Nempe cibus dabatur etiam servis navalibus

If there's an accident, I'm going to charge people to use this exit
Si de caelo cadere incipiamus, vectores pretium pro usu huius exitus poscam

Warning Labels
SCHEDAE MONITORIAE

Your nose may fall off
Fieri potest ut nasus tuus decidat

You may develop hot-dog fingers
Fieri potest ut digiti tui formam tomaculorum sumant

Your head may explode
Fieri potest ut caput tuum displodatur

Your brain may turn to mush
Fieri potest ut cerebrum tuum liquefiat

You may start babbling in Latin
Fieri potest ut Latine blaterare incipias

II
LINGUA LATINA MEDIA
INTERMEDIATE LATIN

Caesar's PowerPoint Presentation

CAESAR TIBI PROPOSITA MAXIMI MOMENTI PRAEFERT

I

Argumentum	***Topic***
Gallia, terra in partes tres divisa	Gaul, a country with three parts
*Cisalpina	*Northern Italy
*Transalpina	*France
*Oblitus sum tertiae	*I forget

II

Consilium	***Plan***
*Visere	*Make a visit
*Videre	*Have a look-see
*Vincere	*Take it over

III

Sequelae	***Follow-up***
*De bello stultum librum scribam	*Write a stupid book about it
*A nonnullis irrumatoribus occidar in Foro	*Get assassinated in the forum by a bunch of assholes
*Acetaria et mensis accipient a me nomina	*Salad and month get named after me

IV

Conclusio	*Conclusions*
*Faciam ut animus meus scrutetur	*Get head examined
*Quid illa femella Cleopatra?	*What about that Cleopatra dame?

My child can beat the crap out of your wimpy honours student **Filius meun puerum tuum studiosum laureatum mollem deverberare potest**
Talk to the hand, the face don't understand **Adloquere manum, facies nescit quid velis**

Top 10 Reasons to Live in the Time of the Caesars

DECEM OPTIMAE RATIONUM CUR IN AEVO CAESARUM VIVERE IUCUNDIUS ESSET

X. Calculus won't be invented for another fifteen hundred years
Calculus differentialis non invenietur intra mille quingentos annorum

IX. When you're late on a rainy day, you can always blame the sundial
Si sub love pluvioso serius advenias, tu culpare semper potes horologium solare

VIII. If you piss off one god, you've still got 600 left
Si deum irrites unum, sescenti tibi iam supersint

VII. Actors are treated like dirt
Histriones foede tractantur

VI. Athletes who complain about their pay end up in an urn
Athletae qui queruntur de mercedibus mox in urnas funduntur

V. Scumbags who get the death penalty think they got off light
Scelesti mortis damnati se leviores poenas pensuros reuntur

IV. The likeliest place to find some pushy Christian preacher is inside a lion
Veri simillimum est, locum in quo praedicatorem Christianum protervum invenies, ventrem leoninum esse

III. The French are an ignorant bunch of servile peasants living in smelly huts, and the Germans are getting their asses kicked
Gens Gallorum inerudita servilis agrestis est, in tuguriis foetidis habitans, et Germani vapulant

II. A healthy diet consists of waiting to see if the food taster dies before having anything to eat
Diaeta salubris est, antequam aliquid cenes, observare an moriatur praegustator

I. Everyone is always dressed for a toga party
Omnès amiciuntur semper togis quasi convivium agitaturi

That Old-Time Religion
ILLA RELIGIO PRISCA

Actually, I'm a born-again pagan
Re vera, cultor denuo renatus deorum Romanorum antiquorum sum

I get to worship whomever I like, including SpongeBob SquarePants
Licet mihi venerari pro deo quemlibet, etiam SpongoRobertum QuadratoBracatum

I always ask myself, What would Julius Caesar do?
Me semper rogo, Quid faceret Iulius Caesar?

No, as far as miracles go, this 'J.C.' never raised the dead, but he certainly lowered a lot of the living
Immo, si de miraculis agitur, ille 'I Ce' nullos mortuos ad vitam revocavit, sed tamen multos vivos ad mortem sane misit

We're having a prayer breakfast down at the rifle range
Ientabimus, precatione facta, in campo manuballistulario

I am a firm believer in tough hate
Mihi persuasum est odisse acerbe

Do unto others, but do it first
Fac hominibus aliis, atqui fac prius

Blessed are the poor, because they leave so much more money for the rest of us
Beati pauperes, quoniam tanto plus pecuniae nobis reliquis relinquunt

Blessed are the meek, because we can cut in front of them in queues
Beati mites, quoniam istis in ordine stantibus anteponere nosmet ipsos possumus

If someone smites you on the cheek, turn the other cheek and see what kind of a smiter he is with a bloody stump
Si quis te percusserit in dexteram maxillam tuam, praebe illi alteram ut possis cognoscere quam fortiter percussurus sit bracchio truncato cruento

Love thy neighbors, and to show you really mean it, send 50,000 heavily armed soldiers to knock on their door and ask in the nicest possible way if they'd like to join your empire
Dilige proximos tuos, utque illis ostendas te re vera diligere, mitte decem legiones quae ianuas pulsent et quam dulcissime ab illis quaerant, num velint in tuum imperium recipi

The theory of evolution is baloney. Everyone knows the whole universe came out of Saturn's nostrils
Theoria Darwiniana evolutionis specierum absurda est. Constat inter omnes universitatem rerum ab naribus Saturni venisse

Of course I can speak in tongues, but I prefer Latin

Sane loqui variis linguis possum sicut Apostoli die Pentecostes, sed malo Latine loqui

Let's say grace: O gods, thank you for permitting us to gobble this food the way Caesar gobbled up half of Europe. Amen.

Precemur. O di, gratias vobis agimus, quod nos sinitis hunc cibum sic devorare quo modo C. Iulius Caesar dimidiam partem Europae devoravit. Finis.

Mob Banter
CAVILLATIO SODALIUM

It fell off the back of a truck, capeesh?
De extremo plaustro excidit; comprehendisne mente quod dico?

You got a problem with that, paysan?
Num de hoc dubitas, compagane?

Whatsamatter you?
Quid te sollicitat?

Fuhgeddaboutit
Eice id ex animo

Geddouttahere
Noli mecum nugari

God forbid, a piano should fall on your head
Dii prohibeant ne clavicinium in caput tuum delabatur

Exactly how fresh is that pepper?
Quam recenter lectum est hoc piper?
It fell off the back of a truck, capeesh?
De extremo plaustro excidit; comprehendisne mente quod dico?

New Age Discourse
SERMO NEOMYSTICUS

Meditate on this, pal
Meditare de hoc, amice

Do you know the yoga position where you put your head between your legs and kiss your ass goodbye?
Scisne schema gymnosophisticum per quod, capite inter femora flexo, iubentur basio valere clunes?

Did a dish of potpourri just catch fire, or did someone light up a joint?
Utrum patella florum siccatorum ignem modo concepit, an aliquis accendit sarcinulam cannabis?

Man, that shit is potent – I am like totally in the subjunctive
Mehercle, illa materia tam valida est ut funditus in modo subiunctivo sim

I've got the munchies! Pizza pizza!
Esurio! Libum Neapolitanum!

Hollywood Latin
SERMO LATINUS ACUIFOLIIS

I love it, I love it, I love it!
Id amo, id amo, id amo!

Make the mother the father, change the cat to a dog, and lose the kid with cancer
Muta matrem in patrem, converte felem in canem, amitte puerum cancerosum

And replace all the love scenes with car chases and set it in the Hamptons instead of the Civil War
Substitue autem persecutiones curriles pro episodiis eroticis, et conloca dramatis actionem in Hamtunis in vicem temporis Belli Civilis Americani

Wait, the girl in the copy room hated it!
Siste, puella in scriptorio xerographico fabulam oderat!

I'm putting it in turnaround
Hoc scriptum in purgatorium committo

Pasadena
Praetermitto

You'll never eat lunch in this town again
Numquam in hoc oppido prandebis iterum

Sushi Bar Chitchat

SERMO IN TABERNA IAPONICA PULPAMENTORUM INCOCTORUM MARINORUM

No mackerel, no eel, and no slab of cold egg crud
Mihi nullus scomber, nulla anguilla, nullum frustum ovorum frictorum frigidorum

When I snap apart the chopsticks, do I make a wish?
Estne mos homini findenti virgulas prehensorias aliquod optatum declarare?

What's the deal with the little strip of green plastic with the fringe on top?
Quapropter in catillum poni solet illa taeniola plastica viridis fimbrata?

More tuna, please, and another California roll
Da mihi plus de thunno, sodes, et alterum volumen Californicum

How do you get the little piece of fish to stick to the rice ball?
Quo modo cogitur segmentulum piscis globo oryzae adhaerere?

Are those knives as sharp as they look?
Suntne illi cultri tam acuti quam esse videntur?

You guys make great cars!
Vos vehicula praestantia fabricamini!

Sorry about those atom bombs!
Me paenitet illorum pyrobolorum atomicorum!

Thank you very much!
Vobis plurimas gratias ago!

Computer Language
SERMO LATINUS COMPUTATORIUS

Download the goddamn file, you bug-ridden piece of shit
Assume plicam damnatam, o tu moles muscaria muscerdarum

If you freeze one more time, you're going straight to the landfill
Si denuo congeles, confestim ibis in fossam purgamentorum

Yeah? Well I've got an error message for you, fuckhead – you're about to be shut down improperly with a sledgehammer
Sicine? Nunc age, tibi nuntium erroris habeo, stuprator – mox improprie sopieris malleolo

Car Talk
DISCEPTATIO DE CURRIBUS

It's a hunk of junk!
Acervus inutilium est!

That car is so ugly, you'd have to put a pork chop on the backseat to get the dog to ride in it
Iste currus tam turpis est ut necesse tibi sit ponere offam porcinam in sede postrema ut persuadeas cani ut vehatur eo

You deserve a smack for buying it!
Eum tam imprudenter comparando meruisti alapam!

If the rattle gets too bad, wear earplugs
Nimium si strepat, indue operimenta tuis auribus

Of course you think you can repair it – you're a moron!
Scilicet putas te currum reficere posse – stipes es!

Whatever it is, it's going to cost you five hundred bucks, if that's what it is
Quodcumque est, Ioachimicis tibi quingentis constabit, siquidem est, quod esse creditur

Try putting it in neutral and pushing it off a cliff
Vide quid eventurum sit si, dinexo ingranagio, currum e scopulo pepuleris

Keep in mind, people in the rearview mirror are even stupider than they appear
Tene memoria, viatores conspectos in speculo retrospicienti stultiores esse quam videntur

And remember, don't drive like my brother!
Et memento, noli agere currum ut frater meus!

B.S.
BUBULUM STERCUS

A coyote whose habitat was destroyed by urban sprawl ate my homework

Suo tractu operto suburbio extenso, canis latrans domicilium meum ingressus praescriptum domesticum mihi devoravit

Due to global warming, my homework spontaneously combusted

Orbe terrarum nimium calefacto combustione hydrogonanthracum, pensum meum domesticum sua sponte flammam concepit

My homework was seized as evidence by mistake by CIA agents in a drug bust at the wrong address

In domum meam perperam incurrentes, vigiles qui exsequuntur usum medicamentorum illicitorum nimis studiosi pensum domesticum pro testimonio iniuste abstulerunt

My homework was forcibly recycled by eco-terrorists

Praescriptum meum domesticum per vim in fibras redactum est a sodalitate quae terrore pro Terra utitur

Due to global warming, my homework spontaneously combusted
Orbe terrarum nimium calefacto combustione hydrogonanthracum, pensum meum domesticum sua sponte flamman concepit
That's a load of bull, and you know it!
Merae fabulae sunt, et eas esse tales scis!

My homework contracted mad homework disease and had to be destroyed

Necesse erat pensum domesticum meum, quod incidit in rabiem pensi deleri

Strict zoning codes enacted by the town board make it illegal for me to work at home

Praescriptis severis de aedificiorum usu decretis a decurionibus municipalibus, mihi non licet operari domi

Because of a lack of international standards, the Supreme Court ruled 5–4 that I had to stop doing my homework immediately

Normis civitati universae deficientibus, quinque ex iudicibus Tribunalis Supremi decreverunt, quattuor negantibus, ut pensum statim deponerem

Small Talk During a Colonoscopy

COLLOCUTIO INTER COLONOSCOPIAM

Now I know how a Muppet feels
Nunc novi quid Manipupa sentiat

Any sign of the trapped miners?
Conspicisne metallicos sepultos?

Are you there yet? Are you there yet? Are you there yet?
Advenistine? Advenistine? Advenistine?

Could you provide me with an affidavit stating that my head is not, in fact, up there?
Potesne mihi testimonium impertire adfirmans caput meum reapse non infixum esse podici?

Medical Confab

CONFABULATIO CUM MEDICO

I'm afraid I have some bad news, doc
Vereor ne tristem tibi nuntium adferam, medice

I've noticed you have no concept of time – I've been waiting for over an hour
Animadverti te nullam notionem temporis habere – nam plus quam unam horam tibi praestolatus sum

Your handwriting on prescriptions is totally illegible and shows signs of dementia
Chirographum tuum quasi demens in medicamentorum praescriptis nemo legere potest

Your manner is oddly distracted
Te geris mirum in modum neglegenter

You have an extremely strange sense of humour
Inusitatissima iocaris

Your fees are insane
Mercedes tuae insanae sunt

I think you have a brain tumour
Puto te tuber in cerebro alere

I'll come by again in a year and see how you're doing
Reveniam ad annum ut cognoscam de valetudine tua

Hang in there!
Perfer et obdura!

Homeland Security
SALUS PATRIAE

I'd open these bills, but I'm afraid they may contain anthrax
Has epistulas debitorum solutionem poscentes aperirem, sed metuo ne bacilli anthracis insint

The bad news is, the Martians have landed and, boy, are they mean; the good news is they hate Arabs and they piss gasoline
Tristis nuntio Martios descendisse et, eheu, truculentos esse, sed laetus nuntio illos odisse Arabes oleumque octanum meiere

If you don't give me this putt, the terrorists win
Nisi mihi hunc puteolum concedis, phobistae vincunt

If I can't get a decent table at a top restaurant on short notice, the terrorists have won
Nisi mensam opimam in popina optima extemplo accumbere possum, phobistae vicerunt

If you won't sleep with me, the terrorists will have won
Nisi mecum concubueris, phobistae vicerint

Get out the duct tape – I'm about to fart!
Effer fasciam adhaesivam – mox pedam!

Useful Phrases for Barbarian Evildoers

LOCUTIONES UTILES MALEFACTORIBUS BARBARIS

I surrender! Please do not fire your catapult!
Me dedo! Quaeso, noli iacere tela ballista!

There is no anti-Roman sentiment here!
Hic nemo est quin Romam amet!

We love your big chariots, fast food, and violent culture!
Amamus vestras currus immanes, cibum festinanter paratum, et cultum saevum!

We hate our wicked and corrupt leaders!
Odimus duces nostros improbos pravosque!

We welcome you as liberators, not conquerors!
Vos non victores, sed liberatores salutamus!

We never liked that dirty old city – it's so much nicer as rubble!
Istam urbem squalidam senescentem numquam dileximus – confracta, multo magis nobis placet!

If you see anything you like, don't hesitate to take it!
Si quid videtis quo delectamini, agite, capite sine mora!

We'd much rather be ruled by a distant emperor, even if he's a nitwit!
Multo malimus ab imperatore remoto regi, etiamsi frutex sit!

We'll be sure to let you know if any Huns come this way!
Curabimus ut sciatis num ulli Hunni appropinquent hac via!

Have a really nice epoch!
Sit vobis aetas felicissima!

Game Boy Chatter

HORTAMINA PUERORUM LUDENTIUM ENCHIRIDIIS LUSORIIS

Taste laser death, alien insect scum!
Oppetite mortem lumine amplificato stimulata emissione radiorum, cimices extraterrestriales foedi!

Eat hot lead, Nazi zombie robot commandos!
Vescimini glandibus plumbi candentis, velites nationalisticosocialistici cadaverosi automatarii!

Feel the keen edge of the sword of doom, no-good, stinking, corpse-eating tomb-ghouls!
Sentite aciem acrem ensis mortiferi, o larvae putidae, o bustirapi nefandi!

I am going to programme a simulation of the Roman Empire and rule it unjustly, cruelly, and incompetently!
Mihi est in animo programmare simulationem imperii Romani quam iniuste, atrociter, imperite regam!

Tax the poor!
Impone vectigalia pauperibus!

Bribe the senators!
Corrumpe pecunia senatores!

Rig the elections!
Falle comitia!

Screw minorities!
Defrauda nationes minores in tua civitate!

Pack the courts with obedient dunces!
Stipa basilicas stipitibus obsequentibus!

Arrest protestors on trumped-up charges!
Infer commenta crimina seditiosis apprehensis!

Invade other countries pretty much at random!
Infer forte temere bellum aliis gentibus!

What could possibly go wrong?
Quid nobis infeliciter fieri potest?

Modern Vatican Latin

SERMO LATINUS HODIERNUS IN VATICANO

My patron saint, Miranda, appeared to me in a vision and told me to remain silent

Patrona mea, Sancta Miranda, apparens mihi somnio me iussit tacere

Whom are you going to believe, me or some snot-nosed little boy, no matter how cute?

Utri vos convenit credere? Mihi, an nescio cui puero parvulo muculento, quamlibet pulchellus sit?

Look, these legal fees are putting quite a dent in the old collection plate

En, mercedes iurisperitorum discum eleemosynarium vero vacuefaciunt

What if I say one million Our Fathers and a couple hundred thousand Hail Marys and we just call it even?

Si Orationum Dominicarum decies centena milia recitabo, Salutationumque Beatae Mariae bis vel ter ducena milia, eritne satis?

On the advice of counsel, I have decided to testify in Latin
Iurisconsultus mihi suasit ut testimonium dicerem Latine

The devil made me do it!
Diabolus me coegit peccare!

Learned Latin for Lovers

SERMO LATINUS DOCTUS – AMATORIBUS

I'm only repeating a query that dates back to the Chaldeans, but may I ask, what is your sign?

Si modo licet mihi te rogare idem quod antiqui Chaldaei suas puellas rogare solebant – quo signo nata es?

I think it was Pliny the Elder – or was it Pliny the Younger? – who first pioneered the concept of self-introduction by way of the purchase of a libation, and it is really in homage to him that I am moved to offer to buy you a drink

Credo Gaium Plinium Secundum Maiorem – aut Gaium Plinium Caecilium Secundum Minorem – instituisse ut vir, qui se notiorem puellae facere vellet, ei aliquid liquoris Lyaei compararet; itaque in commemorationem illius iuvat potiunculam tibi praebere

Cicero phrased it best, and I am merely quoting the master when I am driven to remark, 'Nice tits.'

Hoc Marcus Tullius optime verbis expressit, neque profero alia quam ipsissima verba optimi omnium oratorum cum adsevero te venustas habere mammas

Just as Aeneas inquired of Dido in Book Four of the *Aeneid* after stating his desire to install his obelisk in her temple of love – your place or mine? **A te quaeso, sicut in Aeneidos libro quarto Aeneas, elocutus desiderium erigendi summ obeliscum in templo Venereo Didinis, ab ea quaesivit, tuae domi an meae?**
Go fuck yourself **Futue te ipsum**

In the deathless words of the great philosopher-emperor Marcus Aurelius, of course I will respect you in the morning

Si me decet immortalia verba usurpare Marci Aurelii, imperatoris illustris philosophici, certe apud me in honore eris, cras mane

Just as Aeneas inquired of Dido in Book Four of the *Aeneid* after stating his desire to install his obelisk in her temple of love, your place or mine?

A te quaeso, sicut in Aeneidos libro quarto Aeneas, elocutus desiderium erigendi suum obeliscum in templo Venereo Didonis, ab ea quaesivit, tuae domi an meae?

Classical Kiss-offs
VALEDICTIONES ANTIQUAE

Kiss my basilisk
Basia basiliscum meum

Bite my zither
Morde citharam meam

Lick my licorice stick
Linge bacillum glycyrrhizae meum

Suck my aqueduct
Suge meum aquaeductum

Tune my lap trumpet
Tempera tubam quam in sinu fero

Lollipop my toga lizard
Liguri lacertam quae sub toga mea vivit

Lip-read my trouser scroll
Lege labris volumen inguinale mihi

III
SERMO LATINUS ERUDITUS
ADVANCED LATIN

Useful Syntax
SYNTAXIS UTILIS

IMPERATIVE

Futue te ipsum
Go fuck yourself

IMPERFECT SUBJUNCTIVE EXPRESSING A WISH FOR THE PRESENT

Utinam tete futueres
Would that you would go fuck yourself

FIRST SUPINE EXPRESSING A WISH FOR THE PRESENT WITH VERBS OF MOTION

I fututum te ipsum
Go in order to fuck yourself

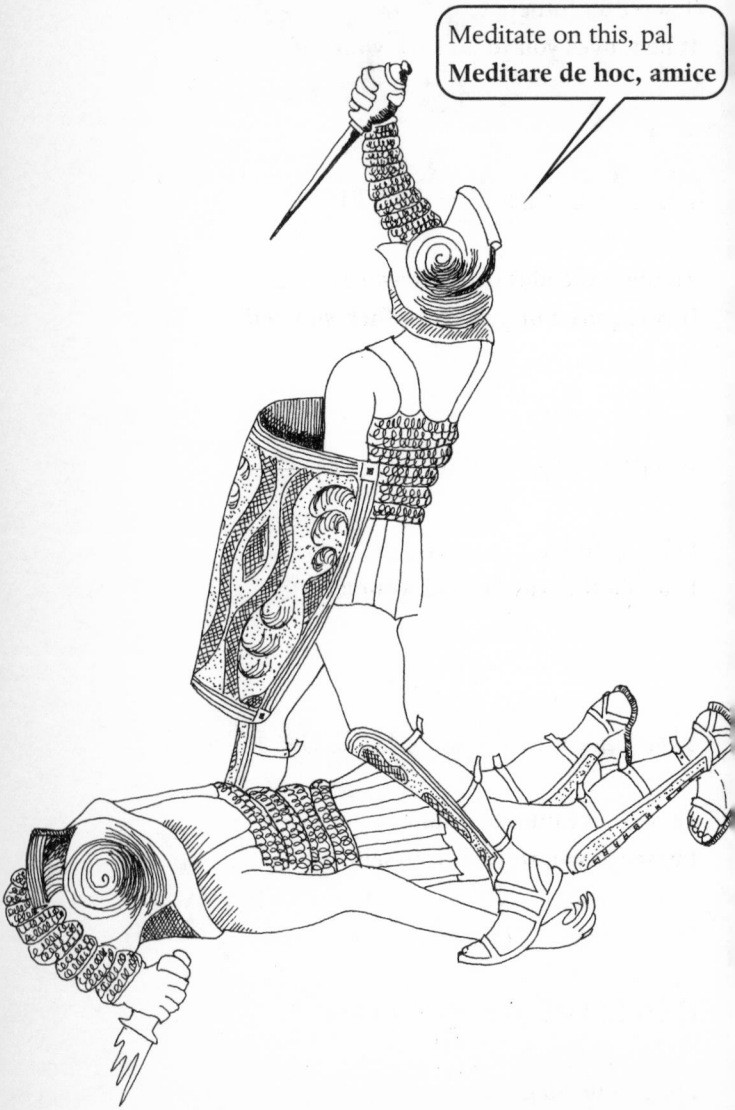
Meditate on this, pal
Meditare de hoc, amice

INFINITIVE WITH IMPERSONAL VERB

Te oportet futuere tete
It behooves you to go fuck yourself

PASSIVE PERIPHRASTIC

Tu tibi futuendus (futuendave) es
It is required of you to go fuck yourself

POTENTIAL SUBJUNCTIVE

Velim te futuas
I should like you to fuck yourself

SUBSTANTIVE CLAUSE OF PURPOSE

Te rogo ut futuas te ipsum
I beseech you to fuck yourself

GENITIVE OF PURPOSE

I tete futuendi gratia
Go for the sake of fucking yourself

FUTURE CONDITIONAL, LESS VIVID

Si te futuas, gaudeam
If you should go fuck yourself, I would rejoice

FUTURE CONDITIONAL, MORE VIVID

Se te futueris gaudebo
If you will have gone and fucked yourself, I will rejoice

PRESENT CONDITIONAL, CONTRARY TO FACT

Si te futueres, gauderem
If you were fucking yourself, I would be rejoicing

PAST CONDITIONAL, CONTRARY TO FACT

Se te futuisses, gavisus (gavisave) essem
If you had fucked yourself, I would have rejoiced

FUTURE PARTICIPLE DENOTING INTENTION OR LIKELIHOOD

Tete fututure, te saluto
You who are about to go fuck yourself, I salute you

FUTURE IMPERATIVE

Tete futuito
Make it your policy to fuck yourself

ABLATIVE ABSOLUTE

Te fututo, gaudeo
You having been fucked, I rejoice

You Know You May Be a Roman If . . .

SCIAS TE FORTASSE ROMANUM ESSE SI . . .

. . . you often forget what you were going to say before you get to the verb

. . . saepe quid habeas in animo dicere priusquam ad verbum pervenias, obliviscaris

. . . you think only superstitious sissies are afraid of volcanoes

. . . credas molles superstitiosos solos timere montes Volcanios

. . . you can eat and have sex at the same time

. . . simul cenare et futuere possis

. . . you have ever used a chariot in a bar fight

. . . umquam in taberna curru proeliatus sis

. . . you never make major business decisions without first cutting open a sheep

. . . numquam de negotio magni momenti decernas sine extispicio

. . . your most recent domestic crisis was a slave revolt

. . . discrimen apud te recentissimum tumultus fuerit servilis

. . . you know anyone who married his own mother or was raised by wolves
. . . quempiam cognoscas qui matrem suam in matrimonium duxerit vel sit a lupis alitus

. . . you have a statue of yourself holding a sword in one hand and the severed head of a Belgian in the other
. . . possideas statuam tui, tenentem manu dextra gladium, manu sinistra caput amputatum Belgae

. . . you compliment the chef by throwing up
. . . coquum vomendo in mensam conlaudes

. . . you have a personal poisoner on your staff
. . . unus ex officialibus tuis propriis est venenarius

. . . the only vegetarian you ever met had hooves
. . . numquam phytophagis occurreris nisi ungulatis

. . . your idea of a party animal is a goat
. . . animal convivialissimum arbitreris esse caprum

. . . your car has sword blades welded to its wheels
. . . habeas currum falcatum

. . . there are usually about three hundred other people in the tub when you take a bath
. . . plerumque, cum laveris, adsint in calidario tecum alii fere trecenti

. . . you think it would be really cool to be Greek
. . . putes esse lepidissimum Graecari

. . . you stay home all day if you see a woodpecker over your left shoulder or hear an owl

. . . domi maneas totum diem cum post tergum conspicias a sinistra picum, vel audias bubonem

. . . you're never surprised to discover that the guy running the empire is a moron, a pervert, or a lunatic

. . . numquam admireris te invenire gubernatorem imperii fatuum esse, vel pravum, vel vesanum

Restaurant 'Tude

BILIS IN POPINA

My name is Sir – I'll be your customer tonight
Nomen mihi est Dominus – hodie vobiscum cenabo

My sign is, I sign the cheque
Natus sum signo signantis syngrapham

The only thing I wish to know about you is where the hell you are when I want something
De te scire volo solum ubi gentium sis cum alicuius indigeam

If those entrées are so special, why aren't they on the menu?
Si quidem illa fercula tantum praestant, cur in epularum indice non sunt?

Exactly how fresh is that pepper?
Quam recenter lectum est hoc piper?

Why do you put it in a mill the size of a war-trumpet?
Quamobrem id ponis in molina tanta quanta tuba est?

This is indeed a very impressive wine list, if you're in the mood for a bottle of grape-flavored rust remover that costs as much as a new sofa

Haec tabula vinorum grandia pollicetur cuicumque sit in animo bibere ex ampulla liquoris qui sapit uvas et solvit ferruginem et stat tanti quanti lectus novus

My compliments to the chef – the empire lost a truly inspired poisoner when he decided to go to cooking school

Summam coquo laudem tribuo – imperium venefico ingeniosissimo privatum est cum ille scholam coquinariam obire statuit

No dessert, thanks, unless it contains the antidote

Benigne, secundam mensam non requiro, nisi antidotum continet

I'd have written in a smaller tip but there is no Roman numeral for a penny

In syngrapha munusculum minus inscripsissem, sed non est littera Romana quae Ioachimici vicesimam significat

I'll be sure to recommend this place to my friends

Zago, zagas, zagat

Winespeak
DICTA ARBITRI VINI

It's an intense chalky white marked by overtones of turpentine and lead, with a bright, long-lasting finish

Vinum peralbum cretosum est, resinam terebinthinam et cerussam redolens, nec sine polimine nitido durabili

It's a pointless little red wine with a unique balance of ignorance and pretension made by an obnoxious millionaire Napa Valley dilettante for self-important dumb-lucky dickheads just like him

Vinum irritum pusillum rubrum est, incomparabiliter librans ignorantiam suam cum ostentatione, a quodam Trimalchione Napaensi confectum salaputiis gloriosis immerito fortunatis, persimilibus sui

It's a dirt-cheap head-banging screw-top bum wine that I poured into a leftover bottle with a fancy French label while no one was looking

Vappa vilissima est, quae capitis dolores facit, quamque ex lagona obturamento versatili clausa in lagunculam reliquam, cui pittacium Gallicum speciosum affixum erat, transfudi, dum nemo me spectabat

Man, that shit is potent – I am like totally in the subjunctive
Mehercle, illa materia tam valida est ut funditus in modo subiunctive sim
It's a dirt-cheap head-banging screw-top bum wine that I poured into a leftover bottle with a fancy French label while no one was looking
Vappa vilissima est, quae capitis dolores facit, quamque ex lagona obturamento versatili clause in lagunculam reliquam, cui pittacium Gallicum speciosum affixum erat, transfudi, dum nemo me spectabat

The Bestseller List
TABULA LIBRORUM VENDIBILISSIMORUM

Quick and Easy Decorating Secrets That Let You Turn a Rustic Hovel into a Charming Country Home without Busting Your Budget by Vitruvius

Artis Ornatus Arcana Per Quae Casa Tua Rustica Celeriter Expediteque Converti Potest in Villam Venustam Sine Sumptu Extra Modum Vitruvius Pollio scripsit

Eat Right – for that Lean and Hungry Look! by Cassius

Edi Recte – ut Speciem Macram et Ieiunam Geras auctore C. Cassio Longino

Great-Tasting Hot Meals Your Slaves Can Whip Up in Two Days or Less by Cato the Elder

Edulia Calida Sapidissimaque quae Familia Tua Potest Parare Duobus Diebus vel Uno M. Porcius Cato descripsit

Cleopatra's Hour-a-Day Bun-Firming Love-Muscle Sexercise Workout by Mark Antony

De Cleopatrae Callipygiana Exercitatione Aphrodisiaca Per Unam Horam in Singulos Dies Musculorum Venereorum M. Antonius scripsit

Letters to My Cat by Pliny the Younger
Epistulae ad Felem Suam quas C. Plinius Caecilius Secundus scripsit

What Colour is Your Catapult? by Frontinus
Cuius Coloris est Catapulta Tua? Sextus Iulius Frontinus scripsit

Oracles Say the Darnedest Things by Livy
Oraculis Inusitatissima Enuntiantur Titus Livius scripsit

Entrail Reading for Dummies by Cicero
Haruspicium Stipitibus Explicat M. Tullius Cicero

Men Are from Troy, Women Are from Greece by Virgil
E Troia Viri, Ex Graecia Feminae Oriuntur P. Virgilius Maro scripsit

Now You Can Lose Weight without Vomiting with the Revolutionary Lark's Tongue Diet by Apicius
Nunc Adipem Deponere Potes Sine Vomitu per Diaetam Novam atque Inauditam Quae Linguarum Alaudarum Esum Praescribit L. Apicius scripsit

Toujours, Gaul by Julius Caesar
Semper, Gallia C. Iulius Caesar scripsit

Latin for Trekkies

SERMO LATINUS SECTATORIBUS PEREGRINATIONIS ASTRALIS

Our shields are down to 25 per cent and those stupid sparks are coming out of all the control panels!

Scutorum nostrorum potestatis remanet solummodo quarta pars, et istae scintillae ridiculae ex omnibus claviaturis gubernatoriis evolant!

We're being controlled by a subordinating conjunction of time implying purpose or intent

Coercemur coniunctione subiunctiva temporali quae propositum vel intentionem significat

Resistance is futile. Prepare to be assimilated into the subjunctive.

Resistere irritum est. Praeparate vos ad translationem in modum subiunctivum.

It's our only hope. Activate the transitive verbs and engage the ablative of separation.

Hoc sola spes nobis est. Verbis transitivis citis, adhibe casum ablativum separationis.

We're entering the future perfect indicative. We'll only have one chance to achieve a case shift.

Intramus tempus futurum perfectum modo indicativo. Unam tantum occasionem habebimus mutandi casum.

We're slipping into the passive. Quick, reroute all available power to the verb endings.

In genus passivum labimur. Inmitte cito impetum omnem quem in promptu habemus in terminationes verborum.

We have entered. We shall have entered! Do be entering!

Intravimus! Intraverimus! Intratote!

To be continued . . .

Narratio resumetur . . .

Attack Ads

PRAECONIUM PROCAX CANDIDATORUM

Ask my opponent why he wants to put a tax on Bibles and American flags to buy gourmet meals for convicted murderers

Quaerite a competitore meo cur vectigal Bibliis Sacris et vexillis Americanis imponere velit ad epulas comparandas homicidis condemnatis

Call my opponent and demand that he stop accepting campaign contributions from operators of nursing-home casinos, publishers of pornographic children's books, and owners of Mexican puppy mills

Vocantes competitorem meum poscite ut desinat accipere ad ambitionem alendam dona vel ab eis qui virginibus puerisque libros edunt Sotadicos, vel ab eis qui aleatoria in gerontocomiis apparant, vel ab eis qui catellos in Hispania Nova immodice alunt

Tell my opponent you oppose his plan to sponsor a law forcing Sunday schools to hire unemployed bilingual homosexual drug addicts

Dicite competitori meo vos obstare proposito suo ferendi legem quae cogat ludos Dominicales conducere paedicatores otiosos bilingues narcomaniacos

Business Latin
SERMO LATINUS NEGOTIALIS

I respectfully decline to answer on the grounds that anything I might say would be a bald-faced lie
Recuso reverenter ne respondeam, quia quicquid dicam id sit mendacium impudens

It wasn't all done with smoke and mirrors – there were some bells and whistles, too
Non solum fumo speculisque, sed etiam tintinnabulis fistulisque factum est

It wasn't really a loss, it was a loan, which of course shows up as a profit
Non vero damnum erat sed mutuum, quod scilicet in rationibus existimatur lucrum

I was out of the loop, but I distinctly remember asking if it passed the smell test
Consilii particeps non eram, tamen memini clare me rogare num id insidias oleret

Due to an alien abduction, I have no recollection of anything else during that particular period of time
Quod raptus sum a transaetheriis, omnia quae evenerunt illo tempore de memoria mea exciderunt

I only sold my stock because a gypsy fortune-teller told me it was an unlucky month for any company with a vowel in its name

Omnes partes meas vendidi tantummodo eo, quod Aegyptia sortilega mihi dixit mensem infaustum esse cuiquam societati quae vocalem in nomine habet

Plus which, I needed cash to buy a condominium for my daughter's hamster

Mihi autem pecunia opus erat ad domicilium emendum criceto filiae meae

I mistook the shredder for a Xerox machine

Discissorem esse Xerographium perperam putavi

Look, let me off the hook and I will rat out every single person in the whole company

Age, da mihi veniam ac impunitatem, deferam unumquemque hominum in societate

Let the buyer go mad
FURAT EMPTOR

Ministerium consultatorium rerum technicarum tibi gratias agit quod vocavisti
Thank you for calling tech support

Verisimile est te haudquaquam intellegere quod dicimus; quid enim?
You probably don't understand a word we're saying; but so what?

Vocatum tuum nullius momenti putamus eumque neglegemus in ordine
Your call is of no interest to us and will be ignored in the order it was received

Fieri potest ut vocatum tuum subauscultemus vel transcribamus animi causa
Your call may be monitored or recorded to provide us with entertainment

Omnes auxiliatores nostri nunc emptores alios furiant
All of our representatives are currently driving other customers crazy

Necesse tibi est morari circa tres dies et dimidiam
Your approximate waiting time is three and one-half days

Preme gullulam primam uti musicam molestam audias
Press one to hear irritating music

Preme secundam ut sonum funis occupati audias
Press two to hear a busy signal

Preme tertiam uti tinnitum sempiternum lineae vacuae audias
Press three for the endless ringing of a non-working extension

Preme quartam uti statim disiungaris
Press four to be immediately disconnected

Sit iucundus tibi dies
Have a nice day

Jury Duty
OFFICIUM IUDICIALE

I'm hopelessly prejudiced – everyone in this court looks like a criminal, including the judge

Opinionem praeiudicatam immutabilem habeo – omnes in hac basilica mihi videri nefarios esse, praetore non excepto

Not fair! Just last month I served as a hooded judge on a secret military tribunal, but they made me promise not to tell.

Iniquum est! Modo proximo mense officio iudicis cucullati functus sum in tribunali clandestino militari tamen coactus sum iurare me de eo taciturum.

I swear to tell the truth, the whole truth, and nothing but the truth, so help, help me Rhonda

Iuro sollemniter me dicturum verum, totum verum, nihil praeter verum, ita me iuvet, iuvet Rhonda

I think I can tell if someone is guilty just by looking at them

Credo me posse diiudicare utrum quis nocens an innocens sit modo eum spectando

If it's really, really close and the jury deadlocks, is it okay to flip a coin?

Si lis valde dubia sit, sententiis iuratorum paribus, liceatne nos nummum iactare, 'caput aut navem' enuntiantes?

If the guy is obviously guilty, can we just skip the trial and send him straight to prison under early admission?

Si reus manifesto sit in culpa, sitne fas nos quaestionem praetereuntes condemnatum in carcerem confestim conicere per admissionem subitariam?

If the gloves don't fit, do we have to acquit?

Si digitalia non congruant manibus, sitne nobis necesse reum absolvere?

Does the jury room have a minibar?

Estne cubiculum deliberationis instructum cistula potionum spirituosarum?

I believe the minimum award in civil cases should be one million dollars, but if you lose, you get the electric chair

Mea sententia, causam privatam obtinenti ut minimum decies centena milia Ioachimicorum addici debent, at de perdente supplicium ultimum in electrica sella sumendum est

I plan to find everyone not guilty by reason of I am extremely pissed off

In animo mihi est, iracundiae meae maximae causa, quemque reum absolvere de crimine

But in a larger sense, can any of us say that we are truly innocent?

Quod autem ad res universas attinet, ecquis nostrum dicere potest se vere innocentem esse?

No, no! It was me! It was me all along! I did it! I did it and I'm glad! Ha-ha, just kidding.

Minime! Non est! Ego fui! Semper ego! Ego facinus feci! Atque gaudeo me fecisse! Hahahae! Tantummodo iocabar.

Stealth Latin
SERMO LATINUS CLANDESTINUS

What you say in Latin
What you say it means
What it really means

Stupra fascino volanti torum pistrinum provolventem
You never cease to amaze me with your deeply insightful remarks
Go take a flying fuck at a rolling doughnut

Quin futuis uxorem tuam foedam?
Why doesn't everyone recognize your genius?
Why don't you go screw your ugly wife?

Velim caput tuum devellere deinde in confinium gulae cacare
I just want to tell you how much I appreciate your constructive criticism
I'd like to rip off your head and take a dump in the hole

Mande merdam et morere
Keep up the good work
Eat shit and die

Propudium parcissimum
I'll get the cheque
You cheap bastard

Carrus exsecrabilis est! Venditor te irrumavit!
What a great car! You got a heck of a deal!
What a piece of shit! You got taken to the cleaners!

Aspice hanc supellectilem vilem. Quale gurgustium est.
Fabulous house – I love your taste.
Look at this cheesy crap. What a dump.

Rotaturne capitulum huius, virus exspuens viride?
Well, now, really, isn't that the cutest baby you've ever seen?
Does its head spin around and spit green slime?

Amica tua est originis extraterrestrialis. Si fortuna tibi faveat, cum astronavem suam ista refecerit, a terra tuaque vita discedet tam cito quam fulmen ascendit.
Your girlfriend is a knockout. Talent, beauty, brains – she has it all.
She's a space alien. If you're lucky, when she gets her flying saucer fixed, she'll be out of here and out of your life in a flash.

Amicus tuus expers rationis est. Viculus nescioquis barone suo privatus est.
Your boyfriend is a great guy. No wonder you've been keeping him to yourself.
He's a total moron. Somewhere there's a village missing its idiot.

Speciem scurrae habes. Spectaculum petauristarum bestiarumque nescieGam adesse.

Dynamite outfit! It really looks good on you.

You look like a clown. I didn't know the circus was in town.

Stealth Latin for Golfers

SERMO LATINUS CLANDESTINUS IN LUSU CALEDONIO

Quod fustuarium!
Nice swing!
What a hack!

Salaputium fortunatum!
Great shot!
You lucky fuckhead.

Seligatur clava imprudenter
Be the right club.
Be the wrong club.

Pilula, curre in harenariam et defode te.
Hurry up ball, get some air! Be there!
Get in that bunker and bury.

Vola! Aberra! Egredere praeter terminos!
Stop! Hit something! Stay in play!
Go! Get lost, ball! Go out of bounds!

Immerge te in aquam!
Stay dry!
Get wet!

Decurre ab area leni in gramen densum!
Sit down! Bite!
Run off the green into the rough!

Transili puteolum!
Go in the hole!
Lip out!

Euax!
Aww, too bad!
Hurray!

Bad Latin, the Dirty Dozen

SERMO LATINUS IMPUDICUS: DUODECIM OBSCENA

asshole	*culus, i* m.; *podex, podicis,* m.
balls	*coleus, i* m.;
to be blown & to blow	*irrumo, irrumare* *fello, fellare;* *ligurio, ire;* *(verpam) comedo, esse, edi, estum*
to bugger	*pedico, are*
butt	*clunis, is* m. & f. *(clunes, ium);* *natis, is* f. *(nates, ium);* *puta, ae* f.
cock	*capulus, i* m.; *cauda, ae* f.; *cicer, is* n.; *clavus, i* m.; *cucumis, eris* m.; *falcula, ae* f.; *fascinum, i* n.; *gladius, i* m.; *hasta, ae* f.; *membrum, i* n.;

mentula, ae f.;
peculium, i n.;
radix, icis, f.;
rutabulum, i n.;
sicula, ae f.;
telum, i n.;
verpa, ae f.;
vomer, eris m.

cunt *aratiuncula, ae* f.;
cunnus, i m.

fart, to fart *crepitus, us.* m.:
strepitus, us m.;
crepo, crepare, crepui, crepitum;
pedo, pedere, pepedi, peditum;
strepito, are

to fuck *concumbo, concumbere, concubui, concubitum;*
futuo, futuere, futui, fututum

to jerk off *frico, fricare, fricui, frictum (fricatum);*
percieo, ire, ivi, itum;
sollicito, are;
tero, terere, trivi, tritum;
tracto, tractare

piss, to piss *urina, ae* f.;
meio, meiere, mixi, mictum;
mingo, mingere, minxi, minctum

shit, to shit *fimus, i* m. & *filmus, i* n.;
merda, ae f.;
stercus, oris n.;
caco, are

Go ahead, punk – make my day
Age, catamite – fac mihi hunc diem felicissimum